"THE **GOAL**
IS NOT TO BE
RIGHT,
BUT TO BE
CLEAR."

FOCUS YOUR LONG-RANGE VISION

IN PART 4 YOU WILL FIND:

- Examples of long-range vivid descriptions from Scripture & culture

- Practical tools to write your own vivid description of your beyond-the-horizon vision

- Understanding your church's "vision factor" to determine the scope of your vision

- Step by step guide to develop background vision

- Immediate action steps for your long-range vision

CHAPTER 12

WHAT ARE YOUR DREAMS BEYOND THE HORIZON?

"I saw a
new heaven
and a new earth..."
APOSTLE JOHN

"I will build a
motor car for the
great multitude..."
HENRY FORD

"Look toward
heaven and number
the stars..."
GOD TO ABRAHAM

"We shall not see
space filled with
weapons of mass
destruction..." **JFK**

THE FOUR IMPERATIVES OF MAKING VISION MOVE

CHAPTER 12

1. **Paint a Picture**
2. **Solve a Problem**
3. **Stir the Heart**
4. **God-Size It**

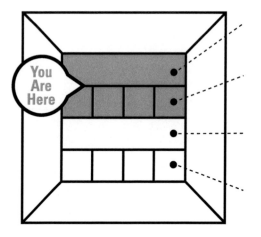

Beyond-the-horizon vision (5-20 years)

Background vision (3 years)

Midground vision (1 year)

Foreground vision (90 days)

WORDS CREATE WORLDS.

Vision travels through people not paper

Vision dripping is more important than vision casting

If your vision doesn't solve a problem it will die on arrival

CALCULATE YOUR VISION FACTOR

$$\frac{M \times Tr \times P}{Tn}$$

M - Culture of Mission

Tr - Dynamic of Trust

P – History of Progress

Tn – Tenure

"The meaning of 'God Size' will flex as you go and grow as a leader."

Your background vision contains four ideas, primarily qualitative, that clarify the four most important strategic emphases in the next three years, in order to fulfill your beyond-the-horizon vision.

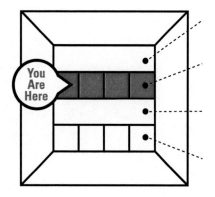

Beyond-the-horizon vision (5-20 years)

Background vision (3 years)

Midground vision (1 year)

Foreground vision (90 days)

You Are Here

"YOUR LONG-RANGE VISION IS THE CONTEXT OF YOUR FUTURE. WHEN YOU ARE DONE CREATING THE CONTEXT, IT'S TIME TO WORK ON YOUR SHORT-RANGE VISION— NEXT YEAR'S COMMITMENT. YOUR CONTEXT WILL DRIVE YOUR COMMITMENT."

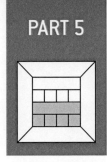

EXECUTE YOUR SHORT-RANGE VISION

IN PART 5 YOU WILL FIND:

- The top 10 reasons for leading with one big goal at a time

- How to develop your midground vision around one measurable goal

- Best practices for focusing your team

- 8 key questions for determining the best goal for your church

CHAPTER 16

TOP 10 REASONS TO HAVE ONE GOAL AT A TIME

9 Connects people to God's larger story of redemptive history

3 Directs everyone's prayers as a concert of dependence

6 Makes momentum easier to generate

1 Focuses the attention of staff and leaders

"THERE ARE NO RESULTS WITHOUT A CONCENTRATION OF RESOURCES."

PETER DRUCKER

CHAPTER

WHAT IS THE SINGLE MOST IMPORTANT PRIORITY FOR THE NEXT YEAR?

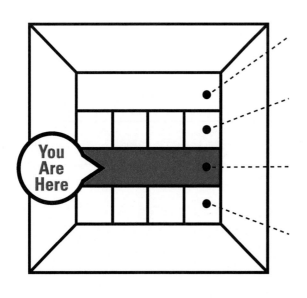

Beyond-the-horizon vision (5-20 years)

Background vision (3 years)

Midground vision (1 year)

Foreground vision (90 days)

90 DAYS
is enough time for
your church to become an
UNSTOPPABLE FORCE
as you implement
your vision.

YOU HAVE 3 KINDS OF FOREGROUND INITIATIVES TO CHOOSE FROM:

1. Cross-functional emphasis
2. Ministry area subgoal
3. All-staff driver

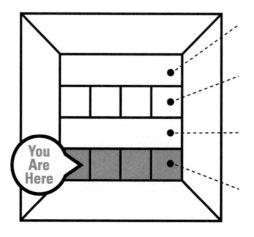

Beyond-the-horizon vision (5-20 years)

Background vision (3 years)

Midground vision (1 year)

Foreground vision (90 days)

You Are Here

USE YOUR HORIZONTAL STORYLINE!

Use your Horizontal Storyline
to share your vision easily, quickly,
and frequently

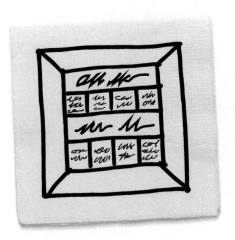

Use your Horizontal Storyline
to train volunteer groups and
leadership teams

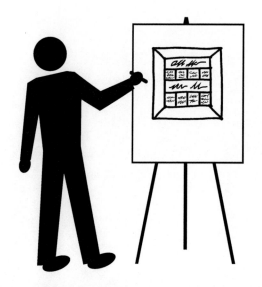

LEAD WITH FREEDOM

IN PART 6 YOU WILL FIND:

- My deepest heartfelt appeal for why you should build a Horizon Storyline with your team

- The 4 greatest benefits of leading with stunning clarity

> "I glorified you on earth by completing the work you gave me to do."
>
> **JESUS**

Made in the USA
San Bernardino, CA
02 May 2017

IN THE END, IT'S ABOUT YOUR FREEDOM.

FREEDOM IS NOT
DOING ANYTHING YOU WANT.
IT'S THE OPPORTUNITY TO
GIVE ALL OF YOURSELF
TO WHAT GOD HAS GIVEN YOU TO DO.

THE HORIZON STORYLINE IS A
WASTE OF TIME
IF IT DOESN'T INJECT
A SENSE OF FREEDOM IN YOUR SOUL

ISBN 9781537263366

9 781537 263366